doctor in the making

A Kids Guide to Becoming a Doctor

sarah michaels

ridiculously simple books

contents

introduction

"Ahoy, young aspiring doctors! Are you ready for the most epic adventure of your life? Well, buckle up, because we're diving straight into the world of medicine! It's going to be a wild ride, filled with tons of laughs, lots of learning, and maybe even a few "Eureka!" moments.

You see, the purpose of this super-duper fantastic book is to give you a sneak peek into the thrilling world of doctors and medicine, but in a way that's as fun as a roller coaster ride! This book is all about guiding you, our brilliant future doctors, on a journey from the classroom to the doctor's office, with a pit stop or two at the laboratory, hospital, and even the mysterious land of Medical School.

We're here to show you that becoming a doctor is not just about memorizing big, fancy words (although there might be a few of those) or wearing a spiffy white coat. Nope, it's also about exploring the wonders of the human body, discovering how to heal and help others, and maybe even saving the day when someone is feeling under the weather.

So, grab your trusty magnifying glass and lab coat, because we're about to embark on an unforgettable adventure into the world of medicine. Together, we'll learn all about what it takes to become a doctor, and who knows, you just might find your calling along the way. So, to sum it up, this book is your golden ticket to a world filled with laughter, learning, and the exciting path to becoming a fantastic doctor!"

hey, you! yes, you: the perfect reader

Listen up, all you cool kids between the ages of 9 and 12, because this book is written especially for YOU! That's right, we're talking about our awesome 5th to 9th graders, who are curious about the world and eager to discover their future paths. Whether you're a science whiz, an aspiring hero, or just someone who loves to learn new things, this book is the perfect fit for your adventurous minds.

Now, don't worry if you're not yet a master of all things medical. This book is designed to be your trusty sidekick as you navigate the twists and turns of the medical world. We've filled these pages with lots of fun, laughter, and entertaining tidbits, all while keeping things at a cool fifth-grade reading level. That way, you can enjoy the journey without getting lost in a sea of big words and complicated jargon.

So, whether you're just starting to explore the incredible world of medicine or you're already dreaming of the day when you'll wear your very own white coat, this book is here to help you every step of the way. And who knows, by the time you're done reading, you might even become the most knowledgeable kid on the block when it comes to all things doctor-related!

In conclusion, this book is like a secret treasure map, designed just for you, our fabulous 5th to 9th-grade readers. And we can't wait for you to start exploring the incredible world of medicine with us. So let's get this adventure started, shall we?

doctor heroes: saving the day, one patient at a time

Picture this: you're walking along, minding your own business, when suddenly – BAM! – you trip and scrape your knee. Ouch! Who do you call? No, not Ghostbusters (although that would be cool). You call a doctor! That's right, doctors are the superheroes of the real world, swooping in to save the day whenever someone is feeling under the weather or battling a nasty case of the sniffles.

But wait, there's more! Doctors don't just fix up boo-boos and chase away colds. They're also super-smart scientists who are constantly learning about the human body and finding new ways to keep us all healthy and strong. From creating powerful medicines to performing life-saving surgeries, doctors are like a mix of Sherlock Holmes, Albert Einstein, and Captain America, all rolled into one.

And let's not forget the most important part: doctors have a huge heart! These caring crusaders dedicate their lives to making people feel better, one patient at a time. They're the ones who hold our hands when we're scared, give us a reassuring smile, and tell us that everything is going to be A-OK. In other words, doctors are the real MVPs of our world, always ready to lend a helping hand (or a stethoscope) whenever we need them.

So, to wrap things up, doctors are kind of like the superheroes of our society, tirelessly working to keep us all happy and healthy. And who knows, maybe one day, you'll be the one wearing the cape (or, you know, the white coat) and saving the day as a marvelous medical hero!

the fantastic voyage: from smarty-pants to super-doc

Hold on to your hats, future doctors, because we're about to take a wild and wacky ride through the process of becoming a doctor! Think of it as a thrilling roller coaster, with twists, turns, and lots of ups and downs (but, you know, the fun kind). So, buckle up, and let's dive into the awesome adventure that awaits all you aspiring medical marvels!

First stop: the world of learning! Yep, you guessed it, doctors need to know a whole bunch of stuff about the human body, diseases, and how to heal people. That means you'll be spending some quality time with your favorite subjects: science, math, and even English. Trust us, knowing how to communicate well is a superpower when you're a doctor!

Next, we'll zoom through the magical land of college and medical school, where you'll transform from a bright-eyed student into a bona fide brainiac! You'll learn all sorts of cool things, like how to diagnose illnesses, perform surgeries, and even save lives. Along the way, you'll meet other aspiring doctors who share your dreams of making the world a healthier place.

But wait, there's more! After medical school, it's time for the ultimate adventure: residency! This is where you'll really hone your doctor skills, working side by side with experienced physicians and learning how to be the best doctor you can be. It's kind of like being a superhero-in-training, preparing for the day when you'll finally get to wear your very own white coat and stethoscope.

So there you have it, the wild and wonderful journey from eager student to super-smart doctor! It's a thrilling ride, filled with learning, laughter, and lots of heart. And as you embark on this fantastic voyage, always remember that you're not just becoming a doctor – you're becoming a superhero in your own right, ready to heal the world and make it a better place, one patient at a time. Onward, future doctors, to your destiny!

1 /
what is a doctor?

doctor, who? decoding the medical mystery

ALRIGHT, future medical masterminds, it's time to put on our detective hats and crack the code of the ultimate question: "What exactly is a doctor?" Is it a mad scientist with a white coat and crazy hair? Or maybe a superhero who can shoot healing rays from their fingertips? Well, not exactly (though that would be pretty cool), but let's dive in and solve this medical mystery together!

A doctor, dear detectives, is a super-smart person who has spent years learning about the human body, health, and how to treat and prevent illnesses. They're like health detectives, piecing together clues and using their brilliant brains to figure out what's ailing someone and how to make them feel better. And just like Batman has his utility belt, doctors have their trusty stethoscopes, prescription pads, and other cool tools to help them save the day.

But here's the twist: not all doctors are the same! That's right, there are many different types of doctors, each with their own special skills and areas of expertise. From pediatricians who take care of kids to surgeons who perform life-saving operations, the world of doctors is as diverse as a bag of jelly beans – each one unique and important in its own way.

So, our daring detectives, we've cracked the case! A doctor is a brilliant, caring, and skilled professional who uses their knowledge and expertise to help people feel better and stay healthy. And as you continue on your journey to join the ranks of these medical marvels, always remember that you, too, have the potential to be an amazing health detective, ready to solve the mysteries of medicine and make the world a better place, one patient at a time. Case closed!

doctor diversity: the wild world of medical marvels

Step right up, future physicians, and prepare to be amazed by the dazzling display of doctor diversity!

That's right, there's a whole world of different types of doctors out there, each with their own unique set of skills and superpowers. So, let's jump into our medical safari and explore some of these fantastic doctor species, shall we?

1. General Practitioners: These are the "jack-of-all-trades" of the doctor world. They can treat a wide variety of illnesses and injuries, from sniffles to sprained ankles. They're like the Swiss Army knives of doctors – always ready with a solution, no matter the problem!

2. Pediatricians: Got a case of the kiddie cold? No problem! Pediatricians are the superheroes of children's health, specializing in treating kids and making them feel better. They're also experts in making funny faces and telling silly jokes to put a smile on their little patients' faces.

3. Surgeons: These doctors are like the magicians of the medical world, performing incredible feats of skill and precision. With their trusty scalpels and steady hands, surgeons can fix broken bones, remove pesky tonsils, and even

mend hearts (both literally and figuratively)!

4. Cardiologists: No, they don't tell fortunes or read tarot cards. Cardiologists are experts in all things related to the heart, from preventing heart disease to treating those pesky, heart-related problems. They're like the "heart whisperers" of the doctor world!

5. Dermatologists: Does your skin need some TLC? Dermatologists are the skin gurus of the medical world, treating everything from itchy rashes to pesky pimples. They're like the fairy godmothers of skin, making sure you always look and feel your best!

And that's just the tip of the iceberg! There are countless other types of doctors out there, each dedicated to helping people in their own unique way. So, as you explore the wild world of medical marvels, remember that there's a doctor for every ailment, a healer for every hurt, and a superhero for every situation. With so many incredible doctors to choose from, the possibilities for your own medical adventure are endless! Onward, future doctors, to the next chapter of our journey!

doctor-patient dream team: the dynamic duo of health

Get ready, future healers, because we're about to explore the incredible, spectacular, and downright amazing role that doctors play in their patients' lives! Picture this: a brave superhero (that's the doctor) and a trusty sidekick (that's the patient) teaming up to fight off evil villains (icky germs and diseases). Sounds pretty cool, right? Well, let's dive into this action-packed adventure and learn more about this dynamic duo!

First up, doctors are like health detectives, using their super-sleuthing skills to figure out what's making their patients feel under the weather. They'll ask questions, perform tests, and examine their patients to gather clues and solve the mystery. It's like a game of "Whodunit," but with germs and bacteria as the sneaky culprits!

Next, doctors become mighty warriors, armed with an arsenal of medicines, treatments, and therapies to help their patients feel better. They'll create a master plan (a.k.a. a treatment plan) to help their patients recover and get back to their healthy, happy selves. It's like watching a superhero movie, with doctors as the caped crusaders saving the day!

But doctors aren't just brainiacs and warriors –

they're also caring and compassionate friends, always there to lend a listening ear or offer a kind word of encouragement. They'll cheer their patients on during their health journey, celebrating victories and offering support during tough times. It's like having your very own cheerleader and life coach, all rolled into one!

So, as you can see, the role of a doctor in a patient's life is nothing short of extraordinary. They're the superheroes, detectives, warriors, and friends that help guide their patients through the wild and wacky world of health. And as you embark on your own journey to become a doctor, always remember that you, too, have the power to be a hero in someone's life, teaming up with your patients to create the ultimate dream team. Adventure awaits, future doctors – let's go!

2 /
preparing for the journey

building blocks of brilliance: the power of a solid start

ATTENTION, future medical masterminds! It's time for some top-secret, super-important advice about the road to becoming a doctor. Are you ready? Here it comes: it's all about the foundation! That's right, just like a mighty skyscraper or a colossal castle, the journey to doctorhood starts with a solid base of education and knowledge. So, grab your hard hats and safety goggles, because we're about to explore the wild world of learning!

First up, we've got the three Rs: reading, 'riting, and 'rithmetic. These are the basic building blocks of your education and will help you develop the skills you need to tackle more advanced subjects later on (like biology, chemistry, and physics – oh my!). Think of these subjects as the sturdy bricks that hold up your tower of knowledge.

Next, we've got your trusty sidekicks: curiosity and creativity. These dynamic duo will help you ask questions, think outside the box, and always be eager to learn new things. They're like the super-glue that holds your educational foundation together, making it even stronger and more resilient.

But wait, there's more! To create a truly unshakable foundation, you'll also need a healthy dose of hard work, determination, and perseverance. These qualities will help you face challenges head-on, conquer obstacles, and never give up on your dreams – no matter how tough things might seem. They're like the steel beams that reinforce your tower of knowledge, making it virtually indestructible.

So, future doctors, as you begin your journey toward medical greatness, always remember the importance of a strong educational foundation. Build your tower of knowledge one brick at a time, and never forget the power of curiosity, creativity, hard work, and determination. With this rock-solid start, you'll be well on your way to becoming the brilliant, world-saving doctors of tomorrow. Now, let's get building!

subject superstars: your path to medical mastery

Alright, future physicians, it's time to roll up our sleeves and get down to business! If you want to become a doctor, there are some seriously spectacular subjects you'll need to focus on. So, strap on your learning cap, grab your trusty pencil, and let's discover the amazing world of subjects that will turn you into medical masterminds!

1. Science Extravaganza: First on our list is the marvelous world of science, which is chock-full of awesome subjects like biology (the study of living things), chemistry (the science of mixing things together to make other things), and physics (the study of how stuff moves and behaves). These subjects are like the golden tickets to understanding the human body and all its fascinating secrets!

2. Math Magic: Grab your calculator and prepare to be amazed, because math is a must-have skill for future doctors! From measuring medicine to calculating doses, math plays a super important role in keeping patients healthy and safe. Plus,

who doesn't love a good math problem to solve during their downtime?

3. Language Arts Lollapalooza: You might be wondering, "What do words have to do with being a doctor?" Well, future healers, language arts are crucial for communicating with patients, writing medical reports, and deciphering the mysterious language of doctor-speak (also known as medical terminology). So, brush up on your grammar, expand your vocabulary, and get ready to become a word wizard!

4. Social Studies Spectacular: Last but not least, social studies help future doctors understand the world and the diverse people in it. By learning about different cultures, beliefs, and ways of life, you'll be better prepared to treat patients from all walks of life with compassion and understanding. Plus, it's always fun to learn about far-off places and fascinating history!

So, there you have it – the superstar subjects that will help you on your journey to becoming a doctor! By focusing on these fantastic fields of study, you'll be well on your way to becoming a medical genius with the power to heal, help, and make the world a healthier, happier place. Now, let's hit the books and conquer the world of learning, one subject at a time!

study power-up: unlocking your inner academic superhero

Hold on to your textbooks, future doctors, because we're about to embark on a thrilling adventure to discover the hidden secrets of powerful study habits! That's right, with the right techniques, you can transform yourself into an unstoppable learning machine. So, grab your favorite highlighter and let's explore the fantastic world of studying like a pro!

1. The Mighty Plan: Just like any great superhero, you need a plan of action to tackle your studies! Schedule regular study sessions and break your learning into manageable chunks. Remember, slow and steady wins the race (or at least helps you ace that biology test)!

2. Study Lair Extravaganza: Every superhero needs a secret lair, and you're no exception! Create a comfortable, quiet, and distraction-free space where you can focus

on your studies. Stock it with all your favorite learning gadgets and gizmos, like colorful pens, sticky notes, and maybe even a cape (for added awesomeness).

3. The Dynamic Duo: Team up with a study buddy to quiz each other, discuss tricky concepts, and practice your newfound knowledge. Two brains are better than one, and together, you'll conquer even the most challenging subjects!

4. Memorization Magic: Unlock the power of mnemonics (memory aids) to help you remember important information. Create silly songs, rhymes, or even dance moves to help those pesky facts stick in your brain like super glue!

5. Power Breaks: Even superheroes need a break from time to time! Schedule short breaks during your study sessions to recharge your brain and give yourself a well-deserved pat on the back. Just make sure you don't get carried away with your break-time dance party (we're looking at you, future cardiologists)!

By mastering these super study habits, you'll be well on your way to becoming the academic superhero you were always meant to be! So, what are you waiting for? It's time to power up, hit the books, and unleash your inner learning legend. Up, up, and away!

extra-fun-ricular: unlocking your hidden superpowers

Listen up, future healers! Being a doctor isn't just about acing exams and mastering medical lingo – it's also about discovering your hidden talents and superpowers through extracurricular activities! That's right, these awesome after-school adventures can help you grow, learn, and have a blast while you're at it. So, let's dive into the wacky world of extracurriculars and learn how they can supercharge your journey to becoming a doctor!

1. Teamwork Triumph: Joining a sports team, drama club, or even a chess club can help you hone your teamwork skills – a must-have for future doctors who need to work together to save lives. Plus, it's a great way to make new friends and have a blast while you're at it!

2. Leadership Legends: By participating in activities like student council or leading a

club, you'll develop the leadership skills needed to take charge and make a difference in the world. Who knows, maybe you'll even become the chief of surgery someday!

3. Creative Crusaders: Unleash your inner artist by joining a band, choir, or art class. These creative pursuits can help you think outside the box and see the world in a whole new way – which is super important for doctors who need to solve complex medical mysteries!

4. Community Champions: Volunteering in your community can teach you about compassion, empathy, and the power of giving back. Plus, you'll get a sneak peek at the real-world impact doctors can have on people's lives, which is sure to give you a warm, fuzzy feeling!

5. Brain-Boosting Bonanza: Enrich your mind with extracurriculars that challenge you intellectually, like a robotics club, debate team, or science fair. These activities will help you sharpen your critical thinking skills, making you an even more brilliant future doctor!

So, future doctors, remember that extracurricular activities are more than just fun and games – they're an essential part of your journey to becoming a well-rounded, world-saving medical superhero! So go on, explore your passions, and let your inner super-powers shine bright. The world is your playground – now go have some fun!

3 /
high school years

course concoctions: mixing up the perfect high school potion

ATTENTION, aspiring medical wizards! It's time to venture into the magical world of high school course selection, where you'll mix together the perfect potion to help you on your journey to becoming a doctor. So, dust off your spell books, grab your wands, and let's get started!

1. The Science Sorcery: To master the mystic arts of medicine, you'll need a strong foundation in science. Sign up for courses in biology (where you'll learn about living things and their cells), chemistry (the potion-making class of the Muggle world),

and physics (the study of forces and energy) to become a true medical magician!

2. Mathemagical Mastery: Even wizards need to know their numbers! Take advanced math courses like algebra, geometry, and calculus to give your brain a workout and help you cast the most powerful healing spells.

3. Literary Lumos: Communication is key in the medical world, so make sure to take challenging English and language arts courses. You'll need to read, write, and speak like a pro to make sure your patients understand the magical remedies you prescribe.

4. Fantastical Foreign Languages: Learning a foreign language can help you connect with patients from all corners of the magical world. Plus, who wouldn't want to impress their friends by casting spells in multiple languages?

5. Enchanting Electives: Don't forget to add some enchanting electives to your potion, like psychology, sociology, or health sciences. These courses can help you explore different aspects of the medical

world and give you a taste of what's to
come in your future career.

So, young wizards, by carefully selecting your high school courses, you'll create the perfect potion to help you on your quest to becoming a doctor. As you mix together science, math, language arts, foreign languages, and enchanting electives, you'll be well on your way to mastering the mystic arts of medicine. Now, go forth and conquer the magical world of high school!

club capers: unleashing your inner extracurricular explorer"

Ahoy, future doctor-adventurers! Are you ready to embark on a thrilling journey through the wild world of clubs and organizations? These fantastic groups offer a treasure trove of opportunities to learn, grow, and discover your hidden talents. So, grab your trusty compass, hoist your sail, and let's set off on an epic extracurricular escapade!

1. Science Swashbucklers: Dive headfirst into
   the realm of science clubs, where you can
   explore the mysteries of the universe,
   conduct awe-inspiring experiments, and

even compete in spectacular science fairs. Who knows what wondrous discoveries await you, future doctors?

2. Math Buccaneers: Plot a course for the math clubs, where you'll sharpen your number-crunching skills, solve perplexing puzzles, and maybe even strike gold in a math competition or two. Arr, matey, math has never been so much fun!

3. Health Heroes: Join forces with other health-focused crusaders in clubs like HOSA (Health Occupations Students of America) or the Red Cross Club. You'll learn about different healthcare careers, practice life-saving skills, and embark on daring missions to help those in need!

4. Creative Crew: Unleash your inner artist by joining a drama, music, or art club. These creative havens will help you think outside the box and see the world in a whole new way – an essential skill for future doctors who need to solve mind-boggling medical mysteries!

5. Volunteering Voyagers: Set sail for the land of community service clubs, where you'll learn the true meaning of giving back. As a future doctor, you'll be a beacon of hope

for those in need – and volunteering clubs
are the perfect place to start!

So, fellow adventurers, by exploring the vast and
exciting world of clubs and organizations, you'll gain
valuable skills, make new friends, and discover your
hidden talents. Now, it's time to weigh anchor, raise
the Jolly Roger, and set off on your epic extracurricular quest. Adventure (and future doctor greatness)
awaits!

doctoring adventures: diving into real-life medical missions

Future doctors, assemble! It's time to embark on a
daring mission into the real world of medicine,
where you'll gain hands-on experience and learn
what it truly takes to become a doctor. So, strap on
your stethoscope, grab your superhero cape, and let's
explore the exciting realm of real-life medical experiences!

1. Shadowing Shenanigans: Team up with a
   real-life doctor for a day of shadowing!
   You'll follow them around, watch them
   work their medical magic, and maybe even
   learn a secret move or two. Just remember,

young sidekick, not all heroes wear capes – some wear white coats!

2. Internship Incredibles: Unleash your inner superhero by landing an internship at a hospital, clinic, or research lab. You'll gain invaluable experience, hone your medical skills, and save the day one patient at a time!

3. Volunteer Ventures: Save the world by volunteering at a local hospital, nursing home, or community health center. You'll learn the power of compassion and empathy – essential superpowers for every future doctor!

4. Medical Missions: Join a medical mission trip or volunteer with organizations like Doctors Without Borders to help provide healthcare to those in need. You'll embark on thrilling adventures, save lives, and make the world a better place – one patient at a time!

5. Medical Camps for Kids: Attend a medical camp designed just for kids, where you'll learn the ins and outs of being a doctor, explore different medical fields, and make new friends who share your passion for healing!

By diving into the thrilling world of real-life medical experiences, you'll gain the skills, knowledge, and confidence you need to become the ultimate medical superhero! So, future doctors, it's time to suit up, step out, and embark on the adventure of a lifetime. The world is waiting, and it's time for you to save the day!

4 /
college preparation

college quest: unraveling the mysteries of higher education"

GREETINGS, brave academic explorers! It's time to embark on an epic quest to uncover the hidden secrets of colleges and universities. With your trusty map and a sense of adventure, you'll navigate the wild world of higher education and discover the perfect school to continue your journey to becoming a doctor. Let the quest begin!

1. College Rankings Riddles: To begin your adventure, decipher the mysterious world of college rankings. Pay special attention to schools with strong medical programs –

these are the legendary temples where you'll unlock the secrets of doctorhood!

2. Location Legends: Just like any great adventure, the setting is key. Consider factors like climate, size, and distance from home when choosing your ideal college. Remember, some explorers prefer bustling cities, while others thrive in peaceful forests – choose the location that feels like your perfect academic playground!

3. Majestic Majors: Uncover the hidden scrolls of various majors and programs. Seek out colleges that offer majors in biology, chemistry, or other pre-med subjects, so you can continue to build your medical knowledge and inch closer to your doctor destiny!

4. Financial Aid Fables: Brave explorer, fear not the dragons of tuition and fees! Seek out the enchanted realm of scholarships, grants, and financial aid to help fund your educational journey. Remember, even the most daring adventurers need a little help sometimes!

5. Campus Chronicles: Immerse yourself in the college experience by visiting campuses, attending open houses, and

talking to current students. Soak up the atmosphere, sample the dining hall cuisine, and imagine yourself as a proud student in these hallowed halls.

By unraveling the mysteries of colleges and universities, you'll find the perfect school to continue your epic journey to becoming a doctor. So, dust off your magnifying glass, sharpen your quill, and set off on your College Quest! The world of higher education awaits, and only you can unlock its secrets!

college crusade: conquering the application battlefield

Fearless future doctors, the time has come to prepare for battle! The college application process is a thrilling yet challenging quest, but with your trusty sword of knowledge and a dash of wit, you'll conquer the battlefield and emerge victorious. So, strap on your armor, hoist your banner, and let's charge into the fray!

1. The Common App Castle: Many colleges use the Common Application – a fortress of forms and essays that streamline the application process. Conquer this mighty

stronghold by gathering your academic records, extracurricular achievements, and a list of schools you'll be applying to. Victory is within reach!

2. Essay Expedition: Pen a powerful, personal essay that tells your unique story. Use your creativity, humor, and wit to win the hearts and minds of college admissions officers. Remember, a well-crafted essay can turn the tide of battle in your favor!

3. Teacher Testimonials: Rally the support of your teachers by requesting heartfelt letters of recommendation. These shining endorsements will bolster your application, proving your worthiness as a future doctor and a noble knight of academia.

4. Standardized Test Siege: Arm yourself with knowledge for the SAT or ACT – two crucial battles in the college application war. Study diligently, sharpen your test-taking skills, and slay these fearsome foes to achieve a high score worthy of your doctor dreams.

5. Application Deadlines Duel: Keep a watchful eye on the approaching deadlines. Submit your applications early

to demonstrate your commitment to the cause and ensure your spot in the ranks of future medical heroes.

By bravely facing the challenges of the college application process, you'll emerge victorious and one step closer to fulfilling your destiny as a doctor. So, raise your banner high, future doctors – the College Crusade awaits! Onward to victory, and may the wisdom be with you!

major mayhem: navigating the wild world of college majors

Attention, scholarly explorers! A new challenge awaits you in the uncharted territory of college majors. But fear not, for your trusty compass of curiosity and a sense of humor will guide you through this wild world. So, lace up your hiking boots, grab your binoculars, and let's embark on the exciting expedition of selecting a college major!

1. Pre-med Pathways: Blaze a trail through the wilderness of pre-med majors like biology, chemistry, or biochemistry. These academic adventures will equip you with

the essential knowledge to tackle the challenges of medical school and beyond.

2. The Wacky Wilderness of Majors: Did you know there's a major called "Puppetry Arts"? While it's tempting to become a puppet master, remember to stay focused on majors that align with your doctor dreams. But hey, feel free to dabble in some creative courses for fun!

3. Double Major Daring: Can't decide between two majors? Combine your passions with a daring double major! Conquer both subjects and emerge as a well-rounded, unstoppable future doctor!

4. Minor Magic: Enhance your major with the enchanting power of a minor! Select a subject that complements your major, like psychology or a foreign language, and dazzle the world with your diverse skills.

5. The Changing Course Conundrum: If you find yourself yearning for a different major, worry not! Many explorers change their paths, and you too can adjust your compass to find the perfect academic adventure.

By navigating the wild world of college majors,

you'll discover the perfect path to support your doctor dreams. So, future doctors, embrace the excitement of the unknown, and let your curiosity guide you through the thrilling expedition of Major Mayhem! The world of academia is yours to explore – go forth and conquer!

5 /
college life

the great juggling act: balancing books and life's buffoonery

LADIES AND GENTLEMEN, boys and girls, welcome to the wacky world of balancing academics and personal life! In this thrilling circus act, you'll play the role of a daring juggler, keeping both your studies and personal interests in the air. So, put on your silliest hat and grab your juggling balls – it's showtime!

1. Time Management Tricks: Master the art of time management, where you'll dazzle the crowd with your ability to juggle schoolwork, extracurriculars, and time for yourself. Create a schedule, prioritize

tasks, and remember – even the best jugglers need a break sometimes!

2. Homework High-Wire: Conquer the tightrope of homework by setting aside a specific time each day to tackle assignments. With practice and balance, you'll complete your schoolwork while still making time for life's little amusements.

3. Extracurricular Escapades: Join clubs and organizations that make you smile, laugh, and feel like you're part of something grand. These wacky adventures will enrich your life, making you a more well-rounded future doctor and a star performer in the circus of life.

4. Laughter and Leisure: Don't forget to take time for yourself to relax, recharge, and revel in life's buffoonery. Whether it's watching funny movies, playing games, or spending time with friends and family, laughter is essential for keeping your juggling act in tip-top shape.

5. The Show Must Go On: When life throws you a curveball, remember to stay flexible and adapt your juggling act. It's okay to drop a ball now and then – the key is to pick it up and keep the show going!

By mastering the great juggling act of balancing academics and personal life, you'll become a superstar in the circus of life, dazzling everyone with your incredible feats. So, future doctors, step into the spotlight and show the world what you've got – it's time to embrace the wild, wacky, and wonderful adventure of The Great Juggling Act!

pre-med party platoon: marching into clubs and organizations

Listen up, future doctors! It's time to enlist in the Pre-med Party Platoon, where you'll join forces with like-minded recruits in pre-med clubs and organizations. So, polish your stethoscope, grab your lab coat, and let's march into the world of pre-med extracurriculars with fun and laughter!

1. Operation Brainy Brigade: Seek out pre-med clubs on campus to connect with fellow students who share your passion for medicine. Together, you'll embark on wacky adventures like dissecting frogs, organizing health fairs, and learning from guest speakers in the medical field.
2. The Laughter League: Join organizations that promote laughter and well-being, such

as comedy clubs, improv troupes, or volunteering at children's hospitals. These groups will help you develop a sense of humor, a skill essential for future doctors and commanders of the Pre-med Party Platoon.

3. Research Reconnaissance: Volunteer for research projects or internships that will immerse you in the world of medicine. Whether it's discovering the secrets of the human body or creating concoctions in a lab, you'll gain valuable experience and some hilarious stories to share with your fellow recruits.

4. Medical Mission Marvels: Participate in medical missions and volunteer opportunities, where you'll provide aid to those in need while gaining hands-on experience. You'll return from these missions with tales of heroism, laughter, and a deeper appreciation for the power of medicine.

5. Pre-med Party Platoon Boot Camp: Attend workshops, conferences, and events focused on medicine and healthcare. These gatherings offer opportunities to learn, network, and share your wacky

medical adventures with fellow future
doctors.

By joining the Pre-med Party Platoon and participating in clubs and organizations, you'll strengthen
your passion for medicine while having a blast. So,
future doctors, rally the troops, and let's march into
the world of pre-med extracurriculars with laughter,
camaraderie, and a sense of adventure! Huzzah!

the great research treasure hunt: unearthing opportunities

Ahoy, future doctors! Ready to embark on a thrilling
treasure hunt to discover the hidden gems of research
opportunities? Grab your trusty map, a sense of
humor, and let's set sail on this swashbuckling
adventure to find your research treasure trove!

1. X Marks the Professor: Start by seeking out
   professors and their research projects.
   Don't be shy, matey – ask about their work,
   and you might find yourself unearthing a
   treasure chest of research opportunities.
2. Department Discovery: Explore the depths
   of your school's science departments,
   where you'll uncover valuable information

about research projects, internships, and lab positions. Keep your eyes peeled, as these gems may be hidden in the most unexpected places.

3. The Internship Island: Chart a course to Internship Island, where you'll find a bountiful selection of research internships in hospitals, laboratories, and research facilities. Just beware of the competitive pirates looking to snag your coveted treasure!

4. Unraveling the Research Riddles: Attend conferences, workshops, and seminars to learn about cutting-edge research and meet fellow treasure hunters. You never know – the next research opportunity might be hidden behind a clever riddle or a chance encounter with a fellow explorer!

5. Online Odyssey: Set sail on the vast ocean of the internet to find research treasure beyond your wildest dreams. Websites, social media, and online forums are filled with hidden gems, so keep your spyglass handy and your wits about you!

By embarking on The Great Research Treasure Hunt, you'll uncover a wealth of research opportunities that will enrich your journey to becoming a doctor. So, future doctors, hoist the Jolly Roger, grab your sense of humor, and let's set sail on this swashbuckling adventure to find your research treasure trove! Arrrrrr!

professor and advisor all-stars: assembling your dream team

Future doctors, are you ready to recruit your very own all-star team of professors and advisors? Put on your coaching hat, grab your clipboard, and let's start scouting for the MVPs who will guide you on your journey to becoming a medical mastermind!

1. The Icebreaker Inning: The first step in assembling your dream team is breaking the ice. Introduce yourself with a smile and a fun fact, like your favorite pizza topping or the number of times you've watched your favorite medical drama.

2. Hallway Huddle: Catch your professor for a quick chat before or after class. Show genuine interest in their work, and you might be one step closer to securing your all-star mentor.

3. Office Hour Olympics: Attend your professor's office hours to discuss class material or ask for advice on your future medical career. Remember, the more you engage, the stronger your bond will become, and the closer you'll be to winning the mentorship gold medal!

4. The Advisor Draft: When choosing an academic advisor, look for someone with experience in the medical field or who shares your zany sense of humor. Your advisor should be a valuable player on your all-star team, so choose wisely!

5. Team Building Extravaganza: Strengthen your relationships by attending events, workshops, and social gatherings hosted by your professors and advisors. This way, you'll get to know them outside the classroom, and who knows, you might even discover a shared love for wacky medical trivia!

By assembling your Professor and Advisor All-Stars, you'll have a dream team ready to guide you on your journey to becoming a doctor. So, grab your coaching hat, a sense of humor, and let's start scouting for the MVPs who will help you conquer the medical world! Let the games begin!

mcat madness: taming the test with laughter and strategy

Future doctors, are you ready to face the wild and wacky world of the MCAT? Fear not, brave adventurers! With a sprinkle of humor and a dash of strategy, we'll conquer this beast together and pave the way to your medical school dreams!

1. MCAT Munchies: Before you embark on your MCAT quest, fuel up with a hearty breakfast. Remember, a well-fed brain is a happy brain, ready to tackle the twists and turns of the test!

2. The Study Plan Safari: Create a study plan that's as unique as a zebra's stripes. Break your study sessions into bite-sized chunks, and don't forget to include plenty of snack breaks and dance parties to keep your energy levels up!

3. Practice Test Party: Host a practice test party with your fellow pre-med pals. Dress up as your favorite body part or medical instrument and celebrate your progress

together. There's no better way to bond than over shared MCAT madness!

4. Joke Break Jamboree: Feeling the pressure? Take a joke break! Share your favorite doctor jokes or silly medical puns with friends and family to lighten the mood and remind yourself that laughter is the best medicine.

5. Pep Talk Powwow: As test day approaches, gather your support squad for a pep talk powwow. Surround yourself with positivity, and remember that you are a brave, brilliant, and hilarious future doctor ready to conquer the MCAT!

By facing the MCAT madness with laughter and strategy, you'll tame the test and continue on your journey to becoming a doctor. So, future doctors, sharpen your pencils, gather your wits, and let's charge into the wild and wacky world of the MCAT together! Onward!

6 /
medical school applications

medical school matchmaking: finding your perfect med school soulmate

FUTURE DOCTORS, it's time for a medical school matchmaking extravaganza! Will you find your perfect med school soulmate? Grab your magnifying glass, put on your detective hat, and let's start our search for the school that'll make your heart go pitter-patter!

1. Dream School Doodle: Get those creative juices flowing by doodling your dream medical school. Does it have a stethoscope-shaped swimming pool or anatomy-themed cafeteria? Let your imagination run wild!

2. Top-Notch Traits: Make a list of the traits you want in your med school soulmate. Are you looking for a school with a strong research focus or one that specializes in intergalactic medicine? The choice is yours!

3. Fact-Finding Fiesta: Embark on a fact-finding fiesta by visiting medical school websites and collecting information on programs, faculty, and campus life. You might even find some amusing school mascots along the way!

4. Campus Tour Treasure Hunt: When you're ready to explore in person, plan a campus tour treasure hunt! As you visit each school, look for clues that'll help you decide if it's the perfect match for your medical dreams.

5. The Great Med School Debate: Gather your friends and family for a lively med school debate! Present the pros and cons of each school you're considering, and let the audience help you decide which one is the best match for you.

By matchmaking your way through the med school search, you'll find the perfect school that makes your heart race and your future medical career soar! So, grab your detective hat, your magnifying glass, and let's dive into this medical school matchmaking extravaganza! Let the search begin!

mission: med school application - the adventure begins

Future doctors, it's time to embark on a top-secret mission: the med school application adventure! Assemble your gadgets, gather your wits, and prepare for a thrilling journey that'll take you one step closer to your doctor dreams.

1. Personal Statement Shenanigans: Unleash your inner storyteller and write a personal statement that's as unique as a three-headed stethoscope! Share your most hilarious doctor dream moments, and don't be afraid to let your personality shine.

2. Loopy Letter of Recommendation: Enlist your favorite teacher, coach, or secret agent for a loopy letter of recommendation that'll make med school admissions committees sit up and take notice. Remember, the more outrageous, the better!

3. Extracurricular Escapades: Compile a list of your wildest extracurricular escapades, from your time as a lab coat-wearing lizard wrangler to your brief stint as a bandage fashionista. Show off your diverse skills and interests!

4. Application Assembly Line: Create an application assembly line in your top-secret mission headquarters (aka your bedroom). Organize your materials, double-check your documents, and make sure your application is as polished as a doctor's shiny white coat.

5. Deadline Dance Party: Keep track of your med school application deadlines with a countdown calendar and celebrate each submission with a victory dance. The more funky moves, the better!

By tackling the med school application process with humor and gusto, you'll navigate this thrilling adventure with style and flair. So, future doctors, fasten your seatbelts, and let's embark on this top-secret mission! The doctor dream awaits!

doctor-to-be's guide to interview invasions

Future doctors, it's time to channel your inner super-hero and gear up for the next stage of your doctor quest: interview invasions! With these super-secret tips, you'll dazzle med school interviewers and conquer this important mission.

1. The Superhero Stance: Before every interview, strike a superhero pose in front of the mirror to boost your confidence. Remember, you're a future doctor with the power to heal and save lives!

2. Wardrobe Wackiness: Choose an outfit that's professional, yet shows off your quirky style. How about a tie with dancing stethoscopes or a pair of lucky medical socks? The sky's the limit!

3. Mock Interview Madness: Enlist your friends, family, or pet hamster to conduct mock interviews. Test your wit by answering zany questions like, "If you could be any medical instrument, which would you be and why?"

4. Fact Frenzy: Dive into a fact frenzy by researching each med school you're

interviewing with. Armed with fun facts and anecdotes, you'll be ready to impress with your knowledge and enthusiasm.

5. Thank-You Note Nonsense: After each interview, send a silly thank-you note that's sure to leave a lasting impression. Try writing it in rhyme or as a mini comic strip featuring Doctor You!

With these interview invasion tips, you'll be well on your way to acing your med school interviews and soaring into your doctor destiny. So, don your cape, practice your superhero pose, and let the interview invasions begin! To the future doctor-mobile!

the great money hunt: scholarships & financial aid

Budding doctors, grab your magnifying glasses and treasure maps—it's time to embark on the Great Money Hunt! With a little detective work, you'll uncover the secrets of financial aid and scholarships to fund your medical school adventure.

1. Financial Aid Fandango: Master the Financial Aid Fandango by dancing your way through the Free Application for

Federal Student Aid (FAFSA). Fill out the forms to the rhythm of your favorite tunes, and watch the money roll in.

2. Scholarship Scavenger Hunt: Embark on a scholarship scavenger hunt to find hidden treasure. Search high and low (and on the internet) for scholarships that celebrate your weird and wonderful talents—like your ability to diagnose a teddy bear's tummy ache.

3. Local Loot: Keep an eye out for local loot by checking with your school, community organizations, or even your Aunt Gertrude, who might know about scholarships offered to future doctors in your area.

4. Essay Extravaganza: Unleash your inner author and pen hilarious, heartfelt essays that'll make scholarship judges laugh, cry, and reach for their wallets. Write about your dreams of curing hiccups or opening a hospital for stuffed animals.

5. Money Milestones: As you collect financial aid and scholarship money, celebrate your victories by adding shiny gold coins (chocolate or real) to a treasure chest. Watching your loot pile up will

keep you motivated on your Great Money Hunt.

With a little creativity and a dash of determination, you'll conquer the Great Money Hunt and fund your future doctor dreams. So, budding doctors, hoist your sails, grab your treasure maps, and let the Great Money Hunt begin! Yarrr!

7 /
medical school

doctor school diaries: the medical school curriculum

WELCOME to the wacky world of medical school, where future doctors learn the secrets of the human body and how to cure boo-boos, tummy aches, and everything in between! Let's sneak a peek at the medical school curriculum, where you'll learn to be a doctor extraordinaire.

1. Anatomy Antics: In Anatomy Antics, you'll become a human body detective, exploring every bone, muscle, and organ. You'll discover the body's hidden mysteries, like why we have belly buttons and how our brains turn thoughts into actions.

2. Physiology Follies: Get ready to giggle in Physiology Follies, where you'll learn how the body works, from the tip-top of your head to the tippy-toes of your feet. Find out how our hearts beat, our lungs breathe, and our stomachs growl when we're hungry for a midnight snack.

3. Pharmacology Party: Pharmacology Party is all about the science of medicines and how they help us heal. You'll learn to mix up magical potions (okay, medications) to help people feel better, like a wizard in a white coat!

4. Doctor Detective: Play doctor detective as you learn to diagnose patients' ailments by piecing together clues from their symptoms. You'll be like Sherlock Holmes, but with a stethoscope instead of a magnifying glass.

5. Bedside Manner Mania: In Bedside Manner Mania, you'll learn the art of making patients smile, even when they're feeling under the weather. Practice your best knock-knock jokes and silly faces to brighten your future patients' days.

Medical school is a wild ride, filled with laughter,

learning, and the occasional late-night study session. By the time you graduate, you'll be a doctor who can cure the common cold, heal a broken heart, and make your patients giggle with glee. Now that's what we call a prescription for fun!

the spectacular spectrum of doctor specialties

Alright future doctors, are you ready to explore the wondrous world of medical specialties? With so many options, it's like an all-you-can-treat buffet of doctor goodness! Let's take a stroll through the land of medical specialties and see what tickles your fancy.

1. The Pediatric Pro: If you're a fan of high-fives, stickers, and making kids feel better, then you might love being a pediatrician. You'll be like a superhero with a stethoscope, fighting off germs and helping kids grow up strong and healthy.

2. The Bone Whisperer: Orthopedic doctors are the magicians of the skeletal system. They mend broken bones, fix wobbly knees, and help people stand tall. If you've ever dreamed of being a bone-

builder, this might be the specialty
for you!

3. The Heart Helper: Do you have a big
   heart? Then you might enjoy being a
   cardiologist, a doctor who specializes in all
   things heart-related. You'll help keep
   hearts happy, healthy, and pumping to the
   beat of life.

4. The Brainiac: If you're fascinated by the
   noggin, then neurology is right up your
   alley! As a neurologist, you'll explore the
   brain's mysteries, from how we think and
   learn to how we dream about ice cream
   sundaes.

5. The Skin Sleuth: Calling all detective fans,
   dermatology might be your calling! As a
   dermatologist, you'll solve the riddles of
   rashes, pimples, and other skin mysteries.
   No case is too itchy or scratchy for you!

Choosing a specialty is like picking your favorite
flavor of ice cream; there's no wrong choice, and you
can always switch if you find a new favorite. As a
doctor, you'll have the chance to explore many
different areas of medicine and find the one that
makes your heart sing (or your bones dance, or your
skin glow – you get the idea). So put on your

thinking cap and dream big, because the world of doctor specialties is waiting for you!

usmle: the ultimate doctor's challenge

Alright, future docs, imagine this: you're a contestant on a game show called "The United States Medical Licensing Examination," or USMLE for short. Sounds fun, right? Well, buckle up, because this is no ordinary game show. It's a series of epic exams that will put your medical knowledge and skills to the test!

1. Step 1: The Trivia Titan: In the first round of this fantastic doctor showdown, you'll face questions on everything from basic sciences to body systems. But don't worry, all those long nights spent studying will pay off when you become a trivia titan!

2. Step 2: The Clinical Crusader: In round two, you'll dive into the real-world challenges of medicine. This part of the USMLE is split into two sub-rounds: CK (Clinical Knowledge) and CS (Clinical Skills). CK tests your ability to apply medical knowledge, while CS is all about showing off your patient care skills. You'll feel like a medical superhero!

3. Step 3: The Grand Finale: The final round of the USMLE is a thrilling two-day event. You'll tackle questions on patient management, and you'll prove you have what it takes to diagnose, treat, and prevent illnesses. It's like an obstacle course for your brain!

Passing the USMLE is a rite of passage for every aspiring doctor. It's like winning the Super Bowl of medicine, except instead of a trophy, you get a license to practice medicine and help people feel better! So, study hard, young medical warriors, because the USMLE awaits. May the force of knowledge be with you!

the great juggling act: school and personal life

Picture this: you're a tightrope walker, balancing a stack of textbooks in one hand and a big, delicious ice cream cone in the other. Sounds tricky, right? Well, that's kind of like what it's like to balance school and personal life!

1. Time Management Magicians: To be a great juggler, you'll need some time

management tricks up your sleeve. Break your day into chunks and assign tasks to each chunk. Poof! You're a time management magician, making more hours appear in your day!

2. The Homework Hoedown: Homework can be a real party crasher, but what if you turned it into a fun dance? Set a timer and tackle your assignments in short, focused bursts. Then, take a break to do a little victory dance. It's the Homework Hoedown!

3. FOMO Frenzy: Fear of missing out (FOMO) can make it tough to balance school and personal life. But remember, there's a time for work and a time for play. So, tell FOMO to take a hike, because you've got this!

4. The Relaxation Station: All work and no play makes for a very grumpy future doctor. Be sure to take breaks and recharge your batteries. Read a book, go for a walk, or just daydream about the awesome doctor you'll become. Welcome to the Relaxation Station!

5. Squad Goals: Surround yourself with positive, supportive friends who

understand your dreams and goals.
Together, you'll create a dream team that
can tackle anything life throws at you!

Remember, future doctors, balancing school and personal life is like walking a tightrope with textbooks and ice cream. But with a little practice, you'll become a master juggler, keeping everything in perfect harmony. So grab your unicycle and let the juggling begin!

8 /
residency

the doctor's adventure camp

IMAGINE GOING to a super cool camp where you get to learn all the amazing skills you need to become a real-life doctor. That's kind of what a residency is like, except with more white coats and stethoscopes!

1. Doctor Boot Camp: After graduating from medical school, future doctors head to residency, which is like a doctor boot camp. Here, they get hands-on experience treating patients and learning from experienced doctors who show them the ropes.

2. Choose Your Adventure: Just like picking a fun activity at camp, doctors in residency

choose a specialty they're passionate about, such as pediatrics, surgery, or even cardiology (heart stuff!).

3. The Learning Marathon: Residency can last anywhere from 3 to 7 years, depending on the specialty. It might seem like a long time, but remember, doctors are training to take care of people's health, so they need to learn all the tricks of the trade!

4. Sleepover at the Hospital: During residency, doctors sometimes have to work long hours and stay overnight at the hospital. It's kind of like a sleepover with your fellow doctors, except you're also learning and saving lives!

5. The Final Boss: At the end of their residency, doctors face the ultimate challenge: board exams! These super important tests help make sure doctors have all the knowledge and skills they need to practice medicine safely.

So, kiddos, think of a residency as the ultimate adventure camp for doctors, where they learn, grow, and become real-life medical heroes. And who knows, maybe one day you'll be the one rocking a white coat and a stethoscope, ready to save the day!

residency: the doctor's job hunt adventure

You know how sometimes it's a real mission to find that perfect toy or snack at the store? Well, when doctors are ready for their residency, they go on their own quest to find the perfect "job" to train for their chosen specialty!

1. Make a List, Check It Twice: First, future doctors make a list of the residency programs they're most interested in. They need to do some detective work, like Sherlock Holmes, to find out which programs are the best fit for them.

2. Time to Shine: Next, they need to prepare their application, including their CV (a fancy word for a resume), recommendation letters, and personal statements. This is their chance to show off their super-duper doctor skills and all the hard work they've done so far.

3. The Interview Quest: Once their applications are submitted, it's time for interviews! This part is kind of like speed dating, but for doctors. They'll visit different residency programs, meet other

doctors, and have interviews to see if they're a match made in medical heaven.

4. Rank 'Em Up: After all the interviews, future doctors rank their favorite residency programs in order. Meanwhile, the programs rank their favorite candidates, too. It's like a giant matchmaking game for doctors and residency programs!

5. The Big Reveal: On "Match Day," the National Resident Matching Program (NRMP) reveals the results, pairing doctors with their residency programs. It's kind of like finding out if you got the toy you wanted at the store, but way more exciting and life-changing!

So there you have it, folks! The residency application process is a thrilling journey for future doctors to find their perfect training ground. One day, you might be the one going on this epic adventure to become a top-notch doctor and change the world!

the match system: doctor love connection

Ever played a matching game, where you flip cards to find the perfect pair? Well, guess what? The Match system for doctors is kind of like that, but instead of cards, it's about finding the perfect residency program for each future doctor. Let's explore this fantastic matchmaking adventure!

1. The Amazing Race: After applying to residency programs, future doctors and residency programs rank their favorites. It's like a race to find the best match before someone else does!

2. The Matchmaker: The National Resident Matching Program (NRMP) steps in as the ultimate matchmaker, making sure everyone's rankings line up. They're kind of like the Cupid of the medical world, making sure the perfect doctor and residency program pair find each other.

3. The Big Day: On "Match Day," the NRMP reveals the results. It's a day full of excitement and nervous energy, as future doctors find out where they'll be spending the next few years training. It's like a surprise party where everyone gets the best gift – a perfect match!

4. The Happy Dance: When the matches are revealed, there's a lot of cheering, high-fiving, and happy dancing. Just imagine

finding your perfect match in a game, but times a zillion!

5. The Adventure Begins: Once the future doctors know where they're going, they can start planning for the amazing journey ahead. It's like getting ready for a grand adventure with a new team, ready to conquer the world of medicine!

So, there you have it! The Match system is a fascinating way for future doctors and residency programs to find their one true match. Just like in a matching game, when the perfect pair comes together, it's a win-win for everyone involved!

a day in the life: resident edition

Imagine living in a fast-paced world, filled with learning, excitement, and lots of coffee! Welcome to the day-to-day life of a resident doctor! Let's jump into their action-packed world and see what a typical day looks like.

1. Rise and Shine: Residents wake up super early, even before the sun is up! They have to be at the hospital to start their day with a bang. Breakfast? They'll usually grab

something quick – no time for fancy waffles here!

2. Morning Huddle: Next, they gather with their team for morning rounds. It's like a morning meeting, but with doctors, discussing their superhero plans to save lives and conquer medical mysteries!

3. The Learning Game: Throughout the day, residents learn from experienced doctors, also known as attendings. It's like having a wise wizard by their side, teaching them magical healing skills!

4. The Patient Party: Residents spend a lot of time talking to and checking up on their patients. They're like detectives, piecing together clues to solve the puzzle of each person's health.

5. The Break Room Breakdown: When they have a spare moment, residents might catch a break in the break room. They'll chat, grab a snack, or maybe even take a power nap – but don't blink, because it won't last long!

6. The Night Shift Shuffle: Some residents work during the day, while others work the night shift, like nocturnal superheroes! They might switch shifts from time to time,

keeping their bodies and minds on their toes!

7. The Pillow Plunge: Finally, after a long and busy day, residents head home to catch some much-needed Zzz's. They'll recharge their batteries, ready to jump back into action the next day!

So, there you have it – a day in the life of a resident! It's a whirlwind adventure, filled with learning, challenges, and, of course, lots of coffee. But in the end, they're one step closer to becoming the superheroes of the medical world!

self-care: the secret superpower

Hey there, future doctors and superheroes! We've got a top-secret mission for you – taking care of yourself! That's right; self-care is your secret superpower to conquer the world (and your studies) with a smile.

1. Sleep Like a Sloth: Getting enough sleep is super important! Even though sloths sleep around 15 hours a day, you should aim for 8 to 10 hours. Rest up, recharge, and let your brain do its magic while you dream of saving lives.

2. Snack Like a Squirrel: Eating well is essential for keeping your energy levels high. Be a snack-savvy squirrel and munch on brain-boosting foods like fruits, veggies, and nuts. Say goodbye to candy bars and hello to superhero fuel!

3. Move Like a Monkey: Exercise helps you stay fit, focused, and fabulous! Swing through the trees (or your neighborhood) like a monkey, and get your heart pumping. You don't need to run a marathon – just have fun and get moving!

4. Chill Like a Cheetah: You might think cheetahs are always on the go, but they need rest too! Find time to relax and unwind. Read a book, watch a movie, or simply daydream about your future adventures in medicine.

5. Laugh Like a Hyena: Laughter is the best medicine! Be a giggling hyena and find humor in everyday situations. Share a joke, watch a funny video, or make silly faces in the mirror – laughter will keep you feeling happy and healthy!

6. Connect Like a Dolphin: Dolphins are social creatures, and so are humans! Stay connected with friends and family, even

when life gets busy. Chat, play games, or hang out together – your support crew will help you stay strong and motivated!

So, future superheroes, remember that self-care is your secret superpower! Take time to sleep, snack, move, chill, laugh, and connect, and you'll be unstoppable in your quest to conquer the world of medicine! Now, go forth and be awesome!

9 /
becoming a licensed doctor

board certification: the ultimate medical ninja test

HEY THERE, future medical ninjas! After all your training, there's one final challenge to prove your skills – board certification! It's like earning your black belt in the world of medicine. Let's dive into this ultimate test of knowledge and skill.

1. The Big Leagues: Board certification is like joining the major leagues of medicine. It shows that you've mastered your specialty and are ready to deliver top-notch care to patients. Doctors, unite!

2. The Test of Time: To become board certified, you must pass a super-duper

challenging exam. It's like a ninja obstacle course for your brain! Study hard, stay focused, and you'll slice through those questions like a medical samurai.

3. The Never-Ending Quest: Board certification isn't a one-time thing. Oh no, medical ninjas must keep learning and growing to maintain their certification. After all, medicine is constantly evolving, and so must you!

4. The Perks of the Title: Being board certified has its perks. Patients trust you more, hospitals love you, and you might even get extra sprinkles on your ice cream! Okay, maybe not the sprinkles part, but you get the idea.

5. The Specialty Showdown: There are many different specialties to choose from, like pediatrics, cardiology, or even ninja medicine (just kidding, that one doesn't exist... yet). No matter your chosen path, board certification will help you become the ultimate medical ninja!

So, future medical ninjas, as you embark on your journey to become board certified, remember that it's like earning your black belt in medicine. Stay strong, study hard, and never stop learning. With determination and a bit of ninja magic, you'll conquer the world of medicine and save lives! Go forth and be legendary!

state medical licensing: the doctor's driver's license

Hey there, future doctor extraordinaires! You know how you need a driver's license to drive a car? Well, state medical licensing is like a driver's license for doctors! It gives you permission to practice medicine in a specific state. But don't worry, there's no parallel parking involved! Let's explore this world of medical licensing.

1. Different States, Different Rules: Each state in the U.S. has its own set of rules for medical licensing. It's like a giant puzzle, and you have to put the pieces together to practice medicine in the state you choose.

2. The Great Medical Road Trip: Want to practice medicine in multiple states? You'll need a license for each one! It's like collecting state-shaped fridge magnets on a road trip, but way cooler and more useful.

3. The Test of Knowledge: To get a state medical license, you'll need to pass an exam (on top of your board certification!). Think of it as a pop quiz, just a tiny bit more important.

4. The Paperwork Party: Getting a state medical license involves filling out a bunch of forms and submitting them to the state's medical board. It may not be as fun as a pizza party, but hey, becoming a doctor is serious business!

5. The License Renewal Fiesta: Your state medical license won't last forever. You'll need to renew it every so often (depending on your state's rules). Just think of it as an ongoing celebration of your doctor awesomeness!

So there you have it, future doctor extraordinaires! To practice medicine, you'll need to grab your state medical license like a boss. Remember, it's like a driver's license for doctors – but way cooler, because you get to save lives instead of just driving to the grocery store. Now go forth, and prepare for the most epic medical road trip of your life!

doctor adventures: job hunt or practice quest?

Ahoy, future doctor adventurers! Oops, I mean, greetings, my medical masterminds! After all those years of learning, exams, and licensing, it's time to put your super-doctor-powers to use! So, what's next? You can either find a job or start your own practice. Let's dive into the exciting world of doctor adventures!

1. The Job-Seeking Safari: Finding a job as a doctor can be like going on a safari, but instead of spotting wild animals, you're hunting for the perfect hospital or clinic. Keep your eyes peeled and your resume ready, because the adventure awaits!

2. The Networking Ninja: To find the best job opportunities, you'll need to be a networking ninja. Connect with other doctors, attend conferences, and join medical organizations. Just remember, a wise networking ninja never reveals all their secrets!

3. The Practice-Starting Puzzle: If you want to start your own medical practice, get ready to put the pieces of the puzzle together.

You'll need to find a location, hire staff, and manage the business side of things. Oh, and don't forget about the medical part, too!

4. The Money Mystery: Whether you're looking for a job or starting a practice, you'll need to navigate the world of salaries, contracts, and finances. It's like solving a mystery, but the prize is a stable income to fund your superhero doctor lifestyle.

5. The Balancing Act: As a doctor, you'll need to find balance between work and personal life. It's like walking a tightrope, except the only thing at risk is your sanity and happiness – no biggie!

So, future doctor adventurers, whether you decide to embark on a job-seeking safari or dive into the practice-starting puzzle, remember that your doctor adventures have just begun. With your medical skills and determination, you're ready to conquer the world – or at least the world of medicine! Now, go out there and make a difference, one patient at a time!

doctor's school: the never-ending adventure

Hey, brainy buddies! Did you think that becoming a doctor meant the end of your school days? Well, surprise! The adventure continues with continuing education and professional development. Let's explore the wacky world of learning that never ends!

1. The Education Escalator: Just like an escalator, learning keeps going up and up! As a doctor, you'll need to keep your brain sharp by learning about new medical discoveries, techniques, and treatments. You'll be the ultimate smarty-pants!

2. The Conference Conundrum: Imagine a party with tons of doctors, scientists, and medical experts. That's a medical conference! You'll attend these fantastic events to learn, share ideas, and meet other medical masterminds. Can you solve the conference conundrum and leave with even more knowledge?

3. The License Renewal Race: To keep your doctor powers, you'll need to renew your medical license regularly. It's like a race against time, where the finish line is

proving you've got the skills to pay the medical bills. Ready, set, renew!

4. The Certification Chase: As a doctor, you can choose to chase after special certifications in your field. It's like a treasure hunt for shiny new titles, and the prize is being recognized as an expert in your area of medicine. Go for the gold!

5. The Mentorship Marathon: As you grow in your medical career, you can become a mentor to other up-and-coming doctors. You'll pass on your wisdom, guide them through challenges, and make sure they're ready for their own never-ending learning adventure.

So, my clever comrades, even though you've become a doctor, the journey of learning never ends. Embrace the education escalator, conquer the conference conundrum, and complete the mentorship marathon. After all, in the wacky world of medicine, there's always more to discover! Keep on learning, and you'll be the most super-duper doctor around!

10 /
the impact of
doctors on society

doctor's heart: the superpower of caring

HEY THERE, future healers! Being a doctor isn't just about having a big brain – it's also about having a big heart. Let's dive into the world of compassionate care, where kindness is the ultimate superpower!

1. The Empathy Express: All aboard! When you're a doctor, it's important to ride the Empathy Express and put yourself in your patients' shoes. By understanding their feelings and concerns, you can offer comfort and support. Choo-choo, here comes the caring crew!

2. The Listening Ladder: Time to climb the Listening Ladder! Doctors need to listen carefully to their patients' stories, concerns, and questions. Each step up the ladder helps you build trust and show your patients that you truly care. Keep climbing, my attentive amigos!

3. The Magic of Manners: Abracadabra! Good manners can work like magic in making your patients feel comfortable and respected. Remember to say "please" and "thank you," and always treat your patients with kindness. It's a magical recipe for happy healing!

4. The Super Support Squad: As a doctor, you'll be part of a team that provides care and support for your patients. Rally your Super Support Squad, and work together to create a warm and welcoming environment. With teamwork, you'll be unbeatable in the battle for compassionate care!

5. The Laughter Laboratory: Laughter is the best medicine, right? As a doctor, it's important to keep your sense of humor and help your patients smile through tough times. The Laughter Laboratory is

where you can mix up the perfect potion of giggles and guffaws for a healing boost!

So, caring crusaders, remember that a big heart is just as important as a big brain in the world of medicine. Climb the Listening Ladder, work with your Super Support Squad, and whip up laughter potions in your Laughter Laboratory. With your superpower of compassionate care, you'll be the ultimate healer – a true superhero in a white coat!

mysterious medical marvels: unleashing your inner scientist

Greetings, inquisitive investigators! Doctors aren't just incredible healers – they're also brilliant brainiacs who make amazing discoveries to improve medicine. Time to put on your lab coats and goggles, because we're about to explore the world of medical research!

1. The Puzzle Palace: Welcome to the Puzzle Palace, where medical researchers solve complex mysteries about the human body. From finding cures for diseases to inventing new treatments, doctors are like detectives, piecing together clues to make the world a healthier place.

2. The Daring Data Divers: Grab your snorkels and flippers, because medical researchers dive deep into oceans of data! They study patterns and trends to better understand diseases and treatments, making them the ultimate underwater data explorers.

3. The Testing Titans: In the realm of the Testing Titans, doctors design and conduct experiments to test new medicines and treatments. With their lab coats flapping like superhero capes, they work to ensure the safety and effectiveness of new discoveries.

4. The Creative Collaborators: When it comes to medical research, teamwork makes the dream work! Doctors join forces with scientists, engineers, and other experts to create a powerful alliance. Together, the Creative Collaborators develop groundbreaking medical innovations.

5. The Trailblazing Teachers: As medical researchers make new discoveries, they become Trailblazing Teachers, sharing their knowledge with others. Through conferences, articles, and presentations,

they teach fellow doctors and future
generations about their amazing findings.

So, future medical researchers, get ready to dive
into the Puzzle Palace, join the Daring Data Divers,
and collaborate with the Creative Collaborators. As
you uncover new discoveries and teach others, you'll
make the world a healthier, happier place. Grab your
lab coat, goggles, and detective hat – it's time to
unleash your inner scientist and change the world!

doctor doo-gooders: heroes of the community

Hold onto your hats, super-kids, because we're about
to embark on an adventure filled with compassionate
care and community spirit! Doctors don't just hang
out in hospitals and clinics; they also swoop in to
save the day by getting involved in their communities. Let's explore the many ways doctors become
real-life superheroes!

1. The Health Crusaders: Armed with their
   trusty stethoscopes, doctors educate the
   community on how to stay healthy and
   avoid pesky illnesses. They swoop into
   schools, community centers, and local

events to share their knowledge, making them true Health Crusaders!

2. The Wellness Warriors: When disaster strikes, the Wellness Warriors are there to help. These brave doctors volunteer during natural disasters, pandemics, and other emergencies, providing medical care and support to those in need. They're like medical knights in shining armor!

3. The Global Guardians: Doctors sometimes travel to far-off lands to help people in need. As Global Guardians, they work with international organizations to provide medical care and improve health in underserved communities. They're the globe-trotting heroes of the medical world!

4. The Support Squad: The Support Squad knows that sometimes, people need more than just medical care. These empathetic doctors volunteer at shelters, food banks, and other organizations, offering a helping hand and a listening ear to those going through tough times.

5. The Mentor Magicians: The Mentor Magicians pass their wisdom onto the next generation of medical heroes. By mentoring students, they inspire future

doctors to follow in their footsteps and continue the legacy of compassionate care.

As you can see, doctors play a huge role in their communities, both locally and globally. So, future doctors, get ready to join the ranks of the Doctor Doo-Gooders! Whether you become a Health Crusader, Wellness Warrior, or Mentor Magician, you'll be making a difference in the world, one compassionate act at a time. Time to grab your cape and join the adventure!

the health avengers: champions of public health

Alright, junior superheroes, get ready for some ACTION! We're about to uncover the secret lives of doctors as they transform into... The Health Avengers! These incredible medical heroes don't just treat sick patients; they also join forces to protect and improve the health of entire communities! Let's see how they battle the forces of unhealthiness and become champions of public health.

1. The Policy Protectors: With the power of knowledge, the Policy Protectors use their medical expertise to shape rules and laws

that keep people safe and healthy. They team up with lawmakers to create better healthcare systems, promote vaccinations, and banish junk food from schools. Watch out, unhealthy habits; the Policy Protectors are coming for you!

2. The Awareness Ambassadors: The Awareness Ambassadors have a knack for spreading the word about health issues. They use their superpowers of communication to educate people about the importance of regular checkups, proper hygiene, and eating fruits and veggies. No couch potato can resist their inspiring messages!

3. The Clean Air Crusaders: Pollution? Not on their watch! The Clean Air Crusaders fight for cleaner air by promoting eco-friendly practices and advocating for policies that reduce pollution. They're like environmental superheroes, saving the world one breath of fresh air at a time!

4. The Fitness Fanatics: The Fitness Fanatics know that exercise is key to a healthy life. They encourage people to get moving by organizing community fitness events, creating fun exercise programs, and

advocating for more parks and playgrounds. Lace-up your sneakers and join the Fitness Fanatics in their quest for a healthier world!

5. The Mental Health Mavericks: The Mental Health Mavericks understand the importance of a healthy mind. They work to break the stigma surrounding mental health, promote access to mental health services, and teach people how to care for their emotional well-being. Minds everywhere, rejoice!

The Health Avengers are true heroes in the realm of public health. As a future doctor, you too can join their ranks and become a champion for healthier communities. Together, you'll battle the forces of unhealthiness and make the world a better place, one healthy choice at a time. Up, up, and away!

conclusion

dr. dazzle's daring dozen: a recap of the doctor adventure

Ladies and gentlemen, boys and girls, it's time for a grand recap of our thrilling journey to becoming a doctor! So, hold onto your stethoscopes and put on your lab coats as we reminisce about the daring dozen steps we took to join the marvelous world of medicine.

1. College Quest: We embarked on an epic adventure to choose the right college and faced the perilous application process. We emerged victorious and ready to start our higher education journey!

2. Major Mayhem: We bravely navigated the challenges of picking a college major and discovered our passion for biology, chemistry, or even underwater basket weaving (just kidding!).

3. Academic Acrobatics: We learned the art of balancing academics and personal life, becoming masters of time management and expert jugglers of responsibilities.

4. Club Crusaders: We ventured into the realm of pre-med clubs and organizations, forging lifelong friendships and honing our medical skills.

5. Research Rumble: We delved deep into the world of research, unearthing new knowledge and making groundbreaking discoveries.

6. Professor Pals: We built strong relationships with professors and advisors, gaining invaluable wisdom and guidance on our path to medical greatness.

7. MCAT Mania: We conquered the mighty MCAT, proving our knowledge and determination to medical schools everywhere.

8. Medical School Mysteries: We researched and applied to medical schools,

deciphering the secrets of their programs and finding our perfect fit.

9. Interview Intrigue: We mastered the art of interviews, dazzling admissions committees with our charm and wit.

10. Money Matters: We navigated the maze of financial aid and scholarships, securing the funds needed to fuel our doctor dreams.

11. Residency Riddles: We explored the enigmatic world of residencies, discovering what specialty called to us and how to find the right program.

12. Match Marvels: We braved the mysterious Match system, finding our perfect residency program and beginning our journey as true medical professionals.

And there you have it, folks: the daring dozen steps of our incredible adventure to becoming a doctor! As we look back on this epic journey, remember that the road to becoming a doctor is filled with challenges and surprises, but it's also an unforgettable adventure that's well worth the effort. So, future doctors, prepare to embark on your own amazing journey, and may the medical force be with you!

doctor dreamers: a pep talk for future medics

Alright, you bright-eyed, bushy-tailed, aspiring doctors, it's time for a pep talk that's more exciting than a double espresso with extra whipped cream! Being a doctor is no walk in the park (unless you're a park ranger), but I'm here to tell you that it's worth every ounce of effort you put into it.

First things first: believe in yourself! You've got more potential than a brand-new pack of markers or a supercharged rubber band ball. You may face challenges and obstacles, but remember, you're like a medical superhero in the making. No challenge is too big for your super-brain and your can-do attitude!

Secondly, embrace your inner mad scientist. Get curious, ask questions, and explore the wonderful world of medicine. Who knows? You might be the one to discover a new cure or invent a life-saving gadget that would make even James Bond jealous.

Don't forget to surround yourself with a team of supporters, kind of like your own personal Justice League or Avengers. Friends, family, teachers, and mentors can all help you stay on track and reach your goals. Plus, it's always more fun to share your victories with your very own cheer squad.

And finally, remember that the road to becoming a doctor is a marathon, not a sprint. So, buckle up, strap on your running shoes, and get ready for the adventure of a lifetime. There will be highs, lows, and everything in between. But at the end of the day, you'll be a real-life superhero, saving lives and making the world a better place.

So, to all you aspiring doctors out there, remember: You've got the brains, the heart, and the courage to make it happen. Now, go forth and conquer the world of medicine! And always keep in mind, even if you stumble along the way, just like a rubber band ball, you'll bounce back and continue rolling towards your dreams!

medicine's marvelous perks: a peek at the payoff

Hey, future doctors! Have you ever wondered what it's like to have a career in medicine? Sure, it's a lot of hard work, but there are some pretty amazing rewards that come with the territory. Picture yourself as a doctor, wearing a cape and soaring through the skies of success. Let's take a look at some of the incredible things that await you in the world of medicine.

First up, you get to be a real-life superhero! You'll be saving lives and helping people feel better every day. Plus, you get to wear a snazzy white coat and maybe even a stethoscope. Who doesn't want to dress like a superhero?

Next, there's the excitement of discovery. The world of medicine is always changing, and you'll be right on the cutting edge of new treatments and technologies. Imagine being the first person to use a brand-new medical gadget that's as cool as something from a sci-fi movie!

Let's not forget about the warm fuzzies you'll get from helping others. There's nothing quite like seeing a patient's smile when they start to feel better, or the gratitude of a family when you've helped their loved one. You'll have the power to make a difference in people's lives, and that's a pretty fantastic feeling.

And of course, there's the stability and financial security that comes with a career in medicine. Not only will you have a rewarding job, but you'll also be able to provide for yourself and your family. You'll be like a superhero who's also an expert at managing their secret identity's finances!

So, future doctors, as you embark on your journey to a career in medicine, remember that the path might be tough, but the rewards are oh-so-worth it.

You'll be a real-life superhero, a master of discovery, and a champion of warm fuzzies. Plus, you'll have the satisfaction of knowing you're making a positive impact on the world. Now, that's a career worth chasing!

appendices

doctor lingo: a silly guide to serious medical words

Greetings, mini medics! So, you want to learn some fancy-schmancy medical terms? Well, buckle up, because we're about to dive into a world of words that'll make you sound like a bonafide doctor in no time!

1. Anesthesia: No, it's not the latest dance craze. It's a magical potion that makes you feel no pain during surgeries or procedures. Abracadabra, owies be gone!
2. Cardiology: A game of cards? Nope! It's the study of the heart, which is way more exciting than a royal flush.

3. Dermatology: Don't worry, it's not about studying worms! It's all about the skin, which is actually the body's largest organ. Who knew?

4. Gastroenterology: Try saying that five times fast! It's the study of the stomach and intestines, so these docs are experts on your tummy's twists and turns.

5. Hematology: The study of blood and all its marvelous mysteries. Hematologists are like detectives, solving cases involving the red stuff that keeps us alive.

6. Immunology: No, it's not about studying the moon. It's all about the immune system, which is like our body's personal superhero team, fighting off pesky germs and infections.

7. Neurology: This one's all about the brain and the nervous system. Neurologists are like brain wizards, casting spells to solve noggin-related riddles.

8. Oncology: Not about studying onions! Oncologists are doctors who help people fight cancer, which makes them real-life heroes in our book.

9. Ophthalmology: Eye spy with my little eye… a doctor who studies eyes!

Ophthalmologists help us see the world clearly and keep our peepers in tip-top shape.

10. Radiology: Nope, it's not about studying radios. Radiologists use super-cool gadgets like X-rays and MRI machines to take pictures of what's happening inside our bodies.

11. Urology: This one's all about the plumbing system of our bodies – the kidneys, bladder, and everything in between. Urologists make sure everything's flowing smoothly!

So, mini medics, now that you've got a handle on these hilarious-sounding medical terms, you're one step closer to sounding like a real doctor. Just remember, practice makes perfect, so don't be afraid to use these fancy words in your everyday conversations. You'll be impressing your friends and family in no time!

the future of doctoring: what awaits aspiring physicians?

Hey there, future doctors! Are you curious about what the future holds for medical professionals like you? Let's take a peek at what you can expect from the ever-evolving world of medicine.

Job Outlook:

Great news, aspiring healers! The demand for doctors is expected to grow faster than the average for all other professions. As the population gets older, there will be an increasing need for medical care, which means more opportunities for you to save lives and make a difference.

Employment Opportunities:

Doctors can work in a variety of settings. From hospitals and clinics to research facilities and private practices, there's no shortage of places where your medical expertise will be needed. And with telemedicine on the rise, you might even have the chance to treat patients from the comfort of your own home (or secret lair)!

Specialties:

The world of medicine is vast and ever-changing, so you'll have the chance to choose from many exciting specialties. Whether you want to fix broken bones as an orthopedic surgeon, explore the mysteries of the brain as a neurologist, or help little ones grow strong and healthy as a pediatrician, there's a perfect fit for every aspiring doctor.

Salary:

Being a doctor isn't just rewarding for the soul – it

can be pretty sweet for your wallet too! While salaries vary depending on factors like location, experience, and specialty, doctors tend to earn more than many other professions. So, you can look forward to a comfortable lifestyle while you're busy healing the world.

Education and Training:

Becoming a doctor takes hard work and dedication, but the journey is well worth it. You'll need to complete your undergraduate degree, attend medical school, and complete a residency program before you can finally don that white coat. But don't worry – with passion, perseverance, and maybe a few cups of coffee, you'll make it through!

Challenges and Rewards:

Being a doctor isn't always easy. You'll face long hours, high-pressure situations, and plenty of tough decisions. But the rewards of helping patients and making a difference in their lives far outweigh the challenges. Plus, you'll have the opportunity to be a lifelong learner, staying up-to-date on the latest medical advancements and treatments.

So, future doctors, the outlook for your chosen profession is bright! Keep working hard, stay focused on your dreams, and soon enough, you'll be making a positive impact on the world through your medical expertise.

Made in the USA
Las Vegas, NV
01 December 2024

13012517R00069